A Kid's Life in
ANCIENT
ROME

by

Hermione Redshaw

BEARPORT
PUBLISHING

Minneapolis, Minnesota

All images are courtesy of Shutterstock.com, unless otherwise specified. With thanks to Getty Images, Thinkstock Photo, and iStockphoto. Recurring images – YamabikaY, Tartila, TADDEUS, sumkinn, Vlada Young, Gaidamashchuk, pics five, adecvatman, Sabelskaya, dimethylorange, Andrey_Kuzmin. Cover – Gilmanshin, Marti Bug Catcher. 2–3 – S.Borisov. 4–5 – donatas1205, pisaphotography, rangizzz, s_oleg, VaLiza. 6–7 – Anna Violet, BearFotos, ben Bryant, Danilo Ascione, HappyPictures, Krakenimages.com, Oleksandr Polonskyi, pics five. YUCALORA. 8–9 – Charly Morlock, ChiccoDodiFC, Katrina Elena, Photosebia. 10–11 – Bill Perry, Charly Morlock, Massimo Todaro, Oligo22, Stefano Panzeri. 12–13 – Algol, imagoDens, Krakenimages.com, Marcos Mesa Sam Wordley, mgallar, Phant, SpicyTruffel. 14–15 – Ekaterina Zelenova, Inspiring, Kalinin Ilya, Krikkiat, magda, PaniYani, Zhuravlev Andrey. 16–17 –ASTA Concept, Azer Mess, Brenda Kean, PiercarloAbate, Romix Image, Shanvood. 18–19 – Nadzin, padu_foto, Sailko (Wikimedia Commons), Zhuravlev Andrey. 20–21 – ben Bryant, Beniho design, cigdem, David Leshem, Gilmanshin, LAN02, Xseon, Yashkin Ilya, Zhuravlev Andrey. 22–23 – mr.Ilkin, Natvas, Thesamphotography. 24–25 – GoodStudio, mountainpix, shakko (Wikimedia Commons), svetograph. 26–27 – BAZA Production, Bill Perry, BlackMac, Massimo Todaro, Prostock-studio, Yulia Serova. 28–29 – Fevziie, footageclips, FXQuadro, Gilmanshin. 30 – VaLiza.

Library of Congress Cataloging-in-Publication Data is available at www.loc.gov or upon request from the publisher.

ISBN: 979-8-88509-951-6 (hardcover)
ISBN: 979-8-88822-125-9 (paperback)
ISBN: 979-8-88822-271-3 (ebook)

For more information, write to Bearport Publishing, 5357 Penn Avenue South, Minneapolis, MN 55419.

CONTENTS

Being a KID

It's tough being a kid. School days are long. There are so many rules to follow. And your parents make you eat vegetables instead of candy!

But how hard is it, really? If you think being a kid is tough today, imagine what it was like living as a kid in ancient Rome.

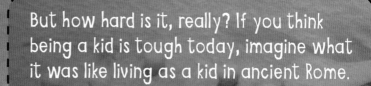

No more peas, PLEASE!!

You'd have school seven days a week, **sewage** would flow down the middle of the street, and vegetables were almost all you'd eat. That's tough!

ANCIENT ROME

Get ready to travel back in time and see what life was like for kids in ancient Rome.

Ancient ROME

The city of Rome was first settled almost 3,000 years ago. Over time, the Romans built a huge **empire** that spread across Europe. They ruled for nearly 1,000 years.

Hello, Europe! You are now part of the Roman Empire!

So much of our world today came from the Roman empire. The ancient Romans built paved roads. They were the first to read books instead of scrolls. And they added January and February to our calendar!

My birthday is in January. Thanks, Romans!

Roman streets may have been paved, but they didn't have sewers yet. So everyone's poop and pee would flow out of the toilets right down the middle of the road. *Yuck!*

I'm not crossing this road!

Instead of paper, ancient Romans wrote on parchment made from animal skins! They used calendars with different names for the months. At first, there were only 10 months with eight-day weeks!

Is it September or Quintilis?

Your guess is as good as mine!

7

SURVIVING
the Time

Your first big challenge as an ancient Roman kid was simple. Just try to survive. That might sound easy. However, ancient Rome could be a deadly place for babies.

What is this soft, crying little blob?

If you made it to your first birthday, well done! You would have survived longer than one out of four Roman babies. However, your parents might seem a little distant. Ancient Romans did not believe babies were fully human yet.

Ma, it's me! Your kid!

If you survived long enough to learn how to walk and talk, you would finally be thought of as a human being.

Now that you are a person, you can learn how to make pots.

Today, doctors and modern **medicine** keep people healthy. Ancient Roman doctors, on the other hand, mostly relied on **herbs** and prayers to keep their patients alive.

Don't worry, sir. Some parsley will probably help.

FAMILIA Faces

In ancient Rome, the family was known as familia. Each familia stuck together and protected one another. If someone went away from their family, they were still part of the familia.

Are we related? You look familia'.

Thanks for adopting me, Dad.

If a Roman had no children to carry on their family name, they would **adopt** a kid. In one case, a man even adopted someone older than him!

No problem, son. Now, get your chores done!

The head of the household was the oldest male. He was known as the paterfamilias, or father of the family. This man had power over everyone else in the family. If he wanted to, he could disown his children!

Don't mess with Dad!

Children had to do what their parents told them to do. You never talked back to your older family members in ancient Rome. Doing so could get you kicked out of the house for good. *Yikes!*

HOME sweet ROME

If you were from a wealthy Roman family, you would live in a domus. This was a house built around a sunny courtyard. A domus had many rooms, including a room with a bath.

Most Romans had to wash in public baths. Going to the bathroom was a **social** event, too. In ancient Rome, people often sat side by side in public toilets.

I think I'll hold it!

Lots of Romans lived in apartment buildings with as many as nine floors—but no elevators! Each apartment had only one or two rooms. You might have to share a bedroom with your parents, grandparents, brothers, and sisters!

There are so many steps!

Cooking was often done in a shared outdoor space, but it wasn't always safe. Roman homes were often at risk of catching fire. One big fire in ancient Rome destroyed many buildings and took six days to put out!

Well, there goes the neighborhood!

SNAIL Salad

Ancient Romans ate lots of vegetables. Cabbage was the favorite of many wealthy Romans. Others could only afford dried peas.

Peas again? I want some cabbage!

I'm off to buy some oranges. See you in a few weeks!

Roman kids couldn't just pick up their favorite fruit at the supermarket. While some fruits grew nearby, others had to be brought from far away. It could be a long journey to get oranges or cherries!

Don't worry! Ancient Roman meals weren't only fruits and vegetables. People sometimes ate bread and meat, too. However, if you're looking for a hamburger, you might be disappointed. Meat was a little bit different back then.

Romans ate meat from rabbits, wild pigs, and ... flamingos! They also ate smaller animals, such as mice and snails. *Yuck!* Those fruits and vegetables probably don't sound so bad now!

Gag!

SINGING
and Sacrifices

The ancient Romans **worshipped** lots of gods and goddesses. They had many of the same gods, myths, and beliefs as the ancient Greeks. However, the Romans gave new names to the older Greek gods.

In Greece, I am Poseidon. But in Rome, they call me Neptune.

Children often took part in **ceremonies** and celebrations for the gods. Sometimes, they sang in choirs. But other times, they had to help **sacrifice** animals. One of those definitely sounds messier than the other....

As a Roman child, you would have to worship statues of gods in your home. You'd even have chores for these household gods. If you didn't do them, bad things might happen to you or your family.

Sweep the floor or you'll be sorry!

Vesta

When lighting a fire in a fireplace, ancient Romans would **honor** the goddess of the **hearth** and home, Vesta. They would often throw something **precious** into the flames.

Why did I have to be precious?

TUNIC
or Not Tunic

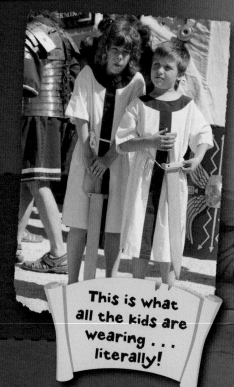

Do you ever wonder what to wear when you wake up in the morning? Well, children in ancient Rome didn't have that problem. They had only one choice of outfit.

This is what all the kids are wearing . . . literally!

I can't wait for shorts and T-shirts to be invented!

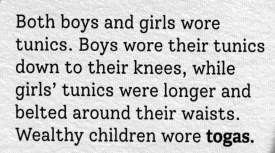

Both boys and girls wore tunics. Boys wore their tunics down to their knees, while girls' tunics were longer and belted around their waists. Wealthy children wore **togas.**

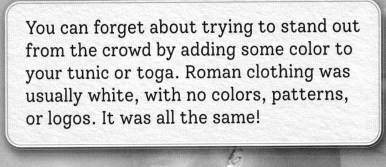

You can forget about trying to stand out from the crowd by adding some color to your tunic or toga. Roman clothing was usually white, with no colors, patterns, or logos. It was all the same!

Children often wore a special **charm** called a bulla that was thought to protect them from evil spirits. Don't lose yours!

A bulla! How charming!

BORED Games

PLAY WITH ME! I'm not creepy!

There were no video games in ancient Rome. Instead, kids would play with dolls and animal figures made from wood, wax, and clay. It must have been hard to snuggle up to a wooden teddy bear!

Ancient Romans also played with bones! One popular game called Knucklebones used small animal bones.

We had mice for dinner, and now I'm ready to play!

The ancient Romans made lots of board games. Some were a lot like games still around today. They had games that were similar to chess, tic-tac-toe, and checkers.

Tabula

I'll trade you my Tabula game for that controller.

Is there really a choice here?

Most Roman toys were educational. They helped kids learn. Roman children also found them entertaining. Then again, they didn't know how cool toys were going to get in about 2,000 years!

Class by CANDLELIGHT

Schools similar to the ones we know today existed in ancient Rome, but they were only for boys. Actually, they were only for boys from wealthy families.

But I'm way smarter than those rich boys!

No fair! I have to go to school every day of the week!

School started before sunrise. There was no electricity, so students had to use candles or oil lamps to see what they were doing. The school day ended in the late afternoon. But you'd be back bright and early the next day. There were no days off!

the plus button?

In school, boys learned reading, writing, and basic math. That might not sound so bad, but their calculators were a little different and their books could be written in either Latin or Greek! Ancient Romans also had to learn how to speak in front of crowds. Hope you like public speaking!

An ancient Roman calculator was known as an abacus.

Do you ever worry about getting a question wrong and looking silly in front of your friends? In ancient Rome, children who gave wrong answers might be beaten in front of the class

Instead of going to a school, some ancient Roman kids had tutors. A teacher would come to their houses. Less wealthy children would often learn the basics from their parents.

This is when the tutor tells my parents I didn't do my homework.

Kids who were taught by their parents might learn how to read and write. But their parents may not have gone to school, either. So, they could teach only what they knew!

mr Dad

I know what I'm talking about!

I'm not so sure.

In school, boys began preparing for their futures by learning how to be warriors. If there wasn't a war being fought by the time they were old enough to be soldiers, they would then be taught how to do their fathers' jobs.

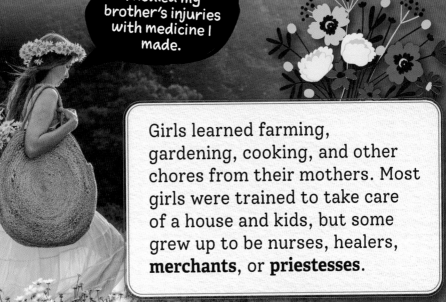

I healed my brother's injuries with medicine I made.

Girls learned farming, gardening, cooking, and other chores from their mothers. Most girls were trained to take care of a house and kids, but some grew up to be nurses, healers, **merchants**, or **priestesses**.

GROWN UP

When?

Being a kid in ancient Rome sounds really tough. Was it better to be an adult? Well, in ancient Rome, you might find out sooner than you'd think!

I can't wait to be a grown-up Roman!

Roman adults kicking back and chilling

Girls were considered women when they were around 12 years old. This usually meant it was time to get married and have kids.

Married? At 12?

In ancient Rome, there was another option for women. Some were chosen to become priestesses. The most important of these were the Vestal Virgins. They lived near the Temple of Vesta and made sure the fire there never went out.

Vestal Virgins worked for 30 years and could not get married during that time. There were only six Vestal Virgins serving at one time. They usually came from rich families.

Boys were thought of as men by around 16 or 17, but they did not always get married right away. That didn't mean they had it easier than girls. Things could get really tough for a boy in ancient Rome.

Tough isn't really my thing.

Once boys became men, they would usually work. This might mean helping their dads or joining the Roman army and going off to war. And there were lots of wars in ancient Rome.

When I said I wanted to travel, I thought we'd be taking the train.

The Roman army was the largest in the ancient world. The best Roman soldiers were the legionnaires. They signed up for at least 25 years, during which time they could be sent to any part of the large Roman Empire.

Life was tough as a Roman soldier. You might have to march 20 miles (30 km) a day while wearing armor and carrying heavy **equipment**. After a long day of marching, you couldn't rest until you built a camp, including walls, tents, and fires!

Is it nap time yet?

That's TOUGH!

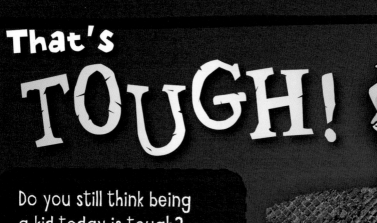

Do you still think being a kid today is tough? At least you don't live in ancient Rome! From mice-and-snail dinners to shared toilet time, it was not a fun time to be a kid!

But don't worry! Your time travel is finished. You no longer need to step over sewage when crossing the street. Now, let's get back to enjoying being a kid here and now.

Which part of life in ancient Rome sounds the toughest?

GLOSSARY

adopt to take into one's family

ceremonies formal events that have special rules

charm an object that has magical powers

empire a group of countries ruled by a leader known as an emperor or empress

equipment tools needed for a special purpose

hearth the area in front of a fireplace

herbs plants or parts of plants

honor to treat someone with respect

medicine something that is used to treat an illness or pain

merchants people who buy and sell things to make money

precious of great value or high price

priestesses women who lead or perform religious ceremonies

sacrifice to offer something of value to a god or gods in order to please them

sewage solid and liquid waste from humans and other animals

social related to a friendly gathering, often with a special purpose or activity

togas loose, draped outer garments worn in public by ancient Romans

worshipped showed respect, love, and devotion

INDEX

READ MORE

Finan, Catherine C. *Ancient Rome (X–treme Facts: Ancient History).* Minneapolis: Bearport Publishing, 2022.

Reynolds, Donna. *Ancient Rome Revealed (Unearthing Ancient Civilizations).* New York: Cavendish Square Publishing, 2022.

LEARN MORE ONLINE

1. Go to **www.factsurfer.com** or scan the QR code below.
2. Enter "**Tough Times Rome**" into the search box.
3. Click on the cover of this book to see a list of websites.